How to Save Time

by
Linda Kita-Bradley

Grass Roots Press

How to Save Time is published by

Grass Roots Press, a division of Literacy Services of Canada Ltd.
Phone: 1-888-303-3213
Website: www.grassrootsbooks.net

ACKNOWLEDGMENTS

We acknowledge the financial support of the Government of Canada through the Canada Book Fund (CBF) for our publishing activities.

Produced with the assistance of the Government of Alberta, Alberta Multimedia Development Fund.

Government of Alberta ■

Editor: Dr. Pat Campbell
Photography: Bev Burke
Book design: Lara Minja, Lime Design Inc.

Library and Archives Canada Cataloguing in Publication

Kita-Bradley, Linda, 1958–
    How to save time / Linda Kita-Bradley.

ISBN 978–1–926583–73–0

    1. Readers for new literates.
2. Readers—Time management. I. Title.

PE1126.N43K58428 2012   428.6'2   C2011–907429–X

Printed in Canada

This is May.

May is busy all the time.

But she gets little done.

So May makes some changes.

May keeps losing her things.

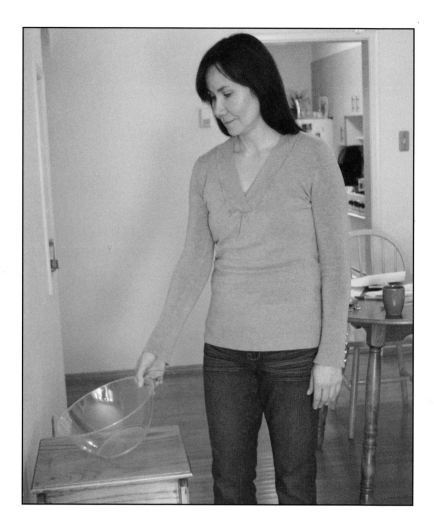

So May puts a bowl on the table.

The bowl holds her glasses.

The bowl holds her keys.

■

The bowl holds her phone.

Now May knows where things are.
May saves time.

May wants to do it all.

May takes classes.

■

She bowls on a team.

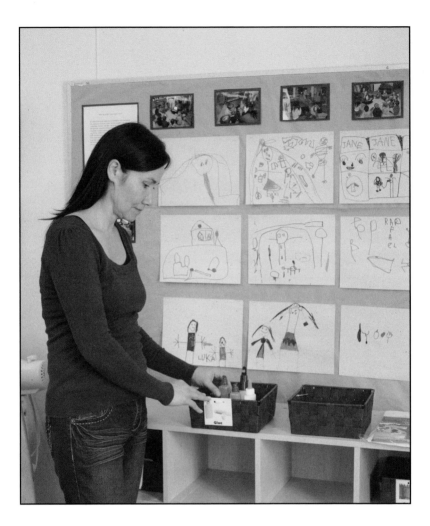

She helps at a play school.

But May cannot do it all.

So May cuts down.
She saves time.

May always has to clean up.

So May talks to her son.
She asks for help.

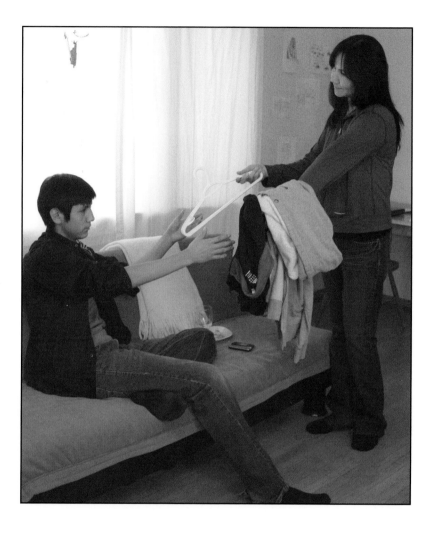

"Please hang up your clothes."

"Please pick up your dishes."

Now May's son helps.
May saves time.

Sometimes, May feels tired.

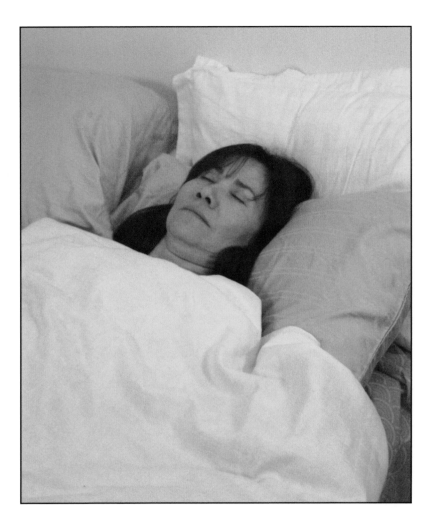

So May tries to sleep more.

May has more energy.

So she gets more done in less time.

May knows how to save time.